Dorset Librarie
Withdrawn Stoc

D0997060

DORSET COUNTY COUNCIL	
205097956 0	
PETERS	£10.99
27-Apr-2010	J538

GRAPHIC SCIENCE

THE ATTRACTIVE STORY OF

MAGNETISM

WITH MAX AXIOM
SUPER SCIENTIST

Andrea Gianopoulos

illustrated by Cynthia Martin and Barbara Schulz

www.raintreepublishers.co.uk
Visit our website to find out
more information about
Raintree books.

To order:
☎ Phone +44 (0) 1865 888066
🖹 Fax +44 (0) 1865 314091
💻 Visit www.raintreepublishers.co.uk

Raintree is an imprint of Capstone Global Library Limited, a company incorporated in England and
Wales having its registered office at 7 Pilgrim Street, London EC4V 6LB
Registered company number: 6695882

"Raintree" is a registered trademark of Pearson Education Limited, under licence to Capstone Global
Library Limited

Text © Capstone Press 2008
First published by Capstone Press in 2008
First published in hardback in the United Kingdom by Capstone Global Library in 2010
The moral rights of the proprietor have been asserted.

All rights reserved. No part of this publication may be reproduced in any form or by any means
(including photocopying or storing it in any medium by electronic means and whether or not transiently
or incidentally to some other use of this publication) without the written permission of the copyright
owner, except in accordance with the provisions of the Copyright, Designs and Patents Act 1988 or
under the terms of a licence issued by the Copyright Licensing Agency, Saffron House, 6--10 Kirby
Street, London EC1N 8T (www.cla.co.uk). Applications for the copyright owner's written permission
should be addressed to the publisher.

ISBN 978 1 4062 1456 7 (hardback)
14 13 12 11 10

British Library Cataloguing in Publication Data
Gianopoulos, Andrea.
Magnetism. -- (Graphic science)
538-dc22
A full catalogue record for this book is available from the British Library.

Art Director and Designer: Bob Lentz
Cover Artist: Tod Smith
Colourist: Krista Ward
UK Editor: Diyan Leake
UK Production: Alison Parsons
Originated by Capstone Global Library
Printed and bound in China by South China Printing Company Limited

Disclaimer
All the Internet addresses (URLs) given in this book were valid at the time of going to press.
However, due to the dynamic nature of the Internet, some addresses may have changed, or sites may
have changed or ceased to exist since publication. While the publisher regrets any inconvenience this
may cause readers, no responsibility for any such changes can be accepted by the publisher.

CONTENTS

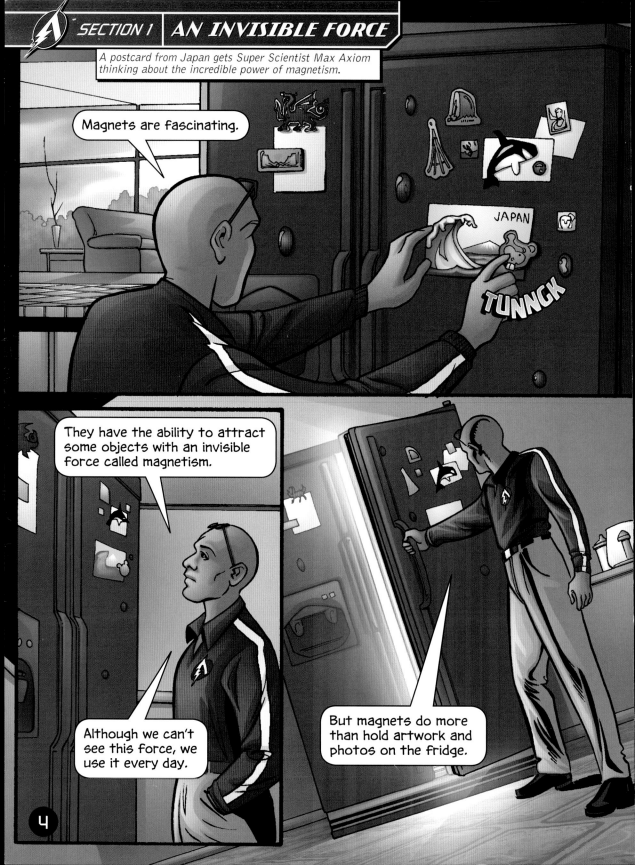

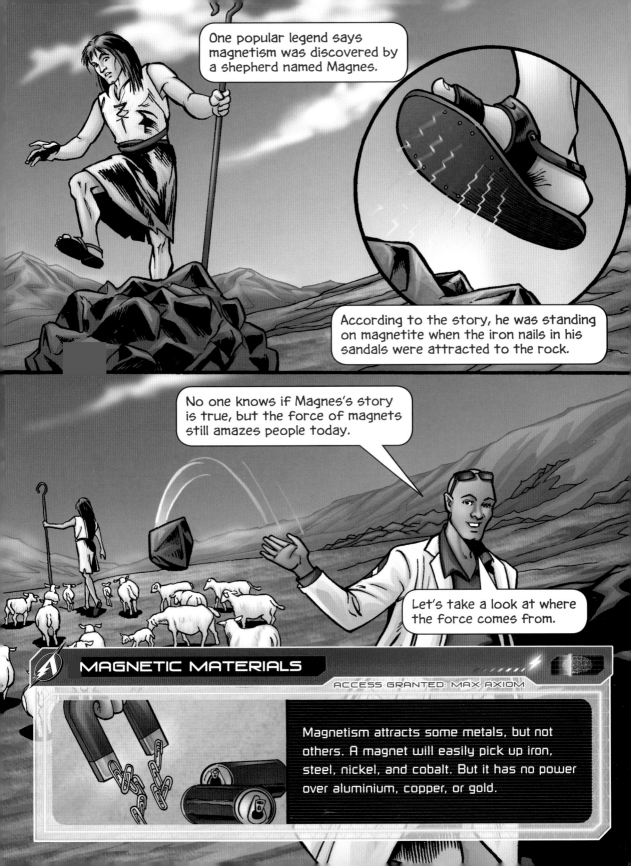

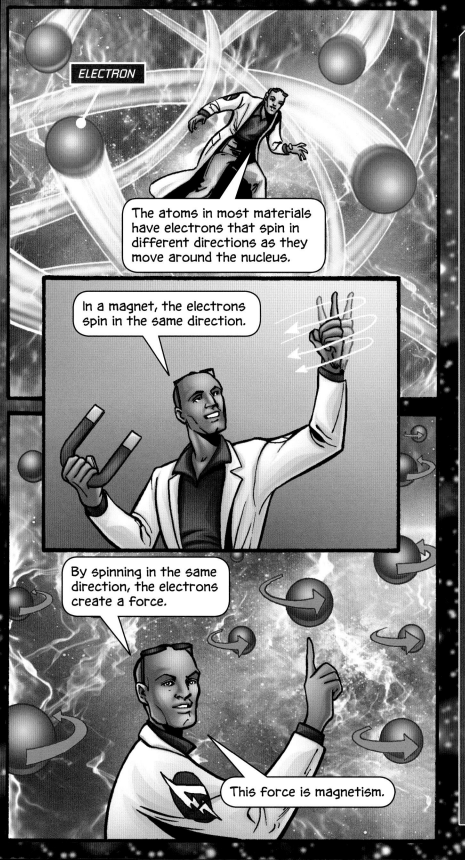

ELECTRON

The atoms in most materials have electrons that spin in different directions as they move around the nucleus.

In a magnet, the electrons spin in the same direction.

By spinning in the same direction, the electrons create a force.

This force is magnetism.

Magnets pass their magnetic power to the objects they attract. A steel washer stuck to a magnet becomes a temporary magnet itself. In fact, a chain of washers can dangle from the magnet as the magnetic force is passed from one washer to the next.

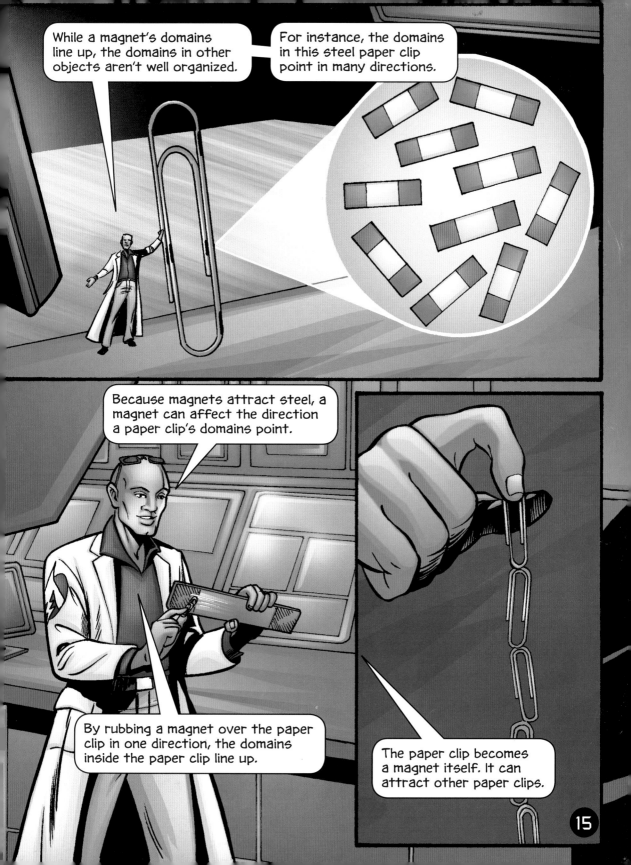

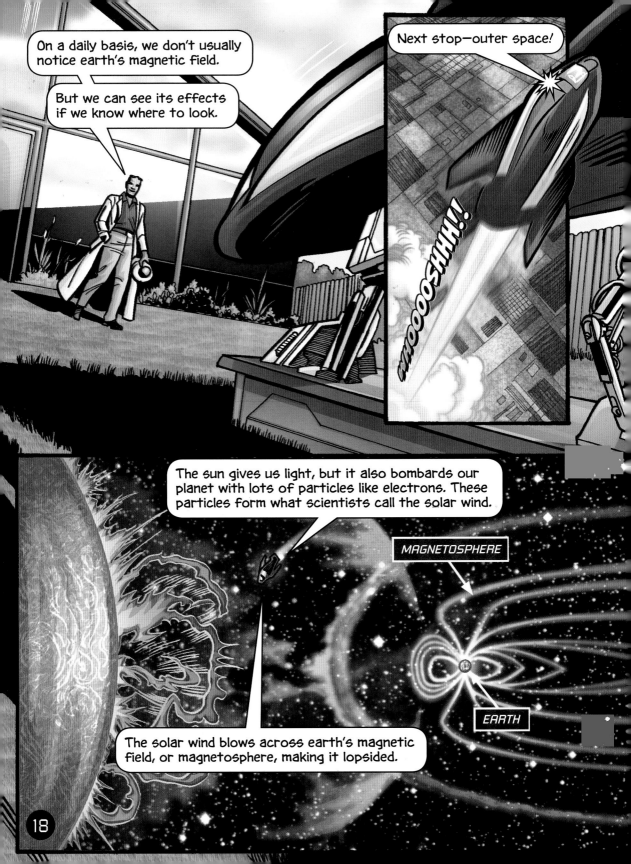

Sometimes the sun shoots off billions of particles in an explosion called a solar flare.

SOLAR FLARE

The particles flood earth's magnetosphere.

VAN ALLEN BELTS

They bounce back and forth between the north and south magnetic poles in an area called the Van Allen Belts.

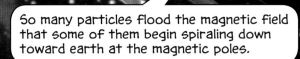

So many particles flood the magnetic field that some of them begin spiraling down toward earth at the magnetic poles.

The particles collide with gases in earth's atmosphere, causing them to glow.

These curtains of colour are called the Aurora Borealis or northern lights and the Aurora Australis or southern lights.

Cranes and maglev trains are examples of big electromagnets in action.

But small electromagnets also run the electric motors of battery-powered toys.

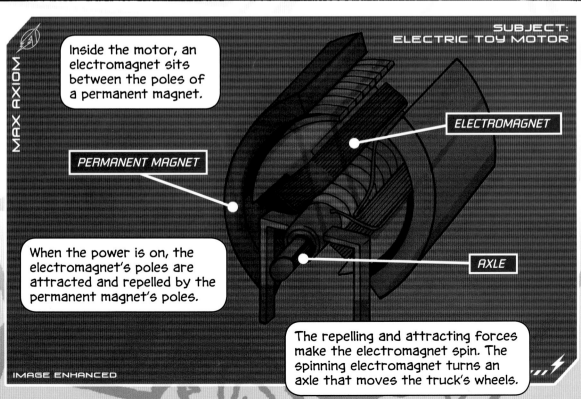

MAX AXIOM

Inside the motor, an electromagnet sits between the poles of a permanent magnet.

ELECTROMAGNET

PERMANENT MAGNET

AXLE

When the power is on, the electromagnet's poles are attracted and repelled by the permanent magnet's poles.

The repelling and attracting forces make the electromagnet spin. The spinning electromagnet turns an axle that moves the truck's wheels.

IMAGE ENHANCED

MORE ABOUT MAGNETISM

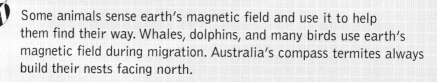

Some animals sense earth's magnetic field and use it to help them find their way. Whales, dolphins, and many birds use earth's magnetic field during migration. Australia's compass termites always build their nests facing north.

Earth's north magnetic pole has moved about 1,125 kilometres (700 miles) since it was first discovered in 1831. If it continues moving at its current speed and direction, the north magnetic pole will be located in Siberia by 2050.

Some farmers make their cattle swallow a magnet to keep them healthy. This small magnet attracts nails and pieces of wire they accidentally eat while grazing. The magnet keeps the bits of metal from passing through their stomachs and damaging their other organs.

The National High Magnetic Field Laboratory at Florida State University in the United States has the world's largest magnet. This giant magnet stands 5 metres (16 feet) tall and weighs more than 13,608 kilograms (30,000 pounds). Scientists developed the magnet for 13 years at a cost of $16.5 million.

The sun has a very strong magnetic field. Over time, this field gets knotted and twisted, creating dark-coloured sunspots on the sun's surface. Sunspots always come in pairs. One is a north magnetic pole while the other is a south magnetic pole.

The sun's magnetic field flips every 11 years. The north magnetic pole becomes a south magnetic pole and the south magnetic pole becomes a north magnetic pole.

 A magnet can attract a British penny. British pennies are made mostly of steel coated with a thin layer of copper. A magnet will easily pick up British pennies because magnets attract steel. However, a magnet won't pick up a United States penny. US pennies are made mostly of zinc and copper. Neither zinc nor copper is magnetic.

MORE ABOUT

SUPER SCIENTIST

Real name: Maxwell Axiom
Height: 1.86 m (6 ft 1 in.)
Weight: 87 kg (13 st. 10 lb.)
Eyes: Brown   Hair: None

Super capabilities: Super intelligence; able to shrink to the size of an atom; sunglasses give X-ray vision; lab coat allows for travel through time and space.

Origin: Since birth, Max Axiom seemed destined for greatness. His mother, a marine biologist, taught her son about the mysteries of the sea. His father, a nuclear physicist and volunteer park warden, showed Max the wonders of the earth and sky.

One day while Max was hiking in the hills, a megacharged lightning bolt struck him with blinding fury. When he awoke, he discovered a new-found energy and set out to learn as much about science as possible. He travelled the globe studying every aspect of the subject. Then he was ready to share his knowledge and new identity with the world. He had become Max Axiom, Super Scientist.

Glossary

atom smallest form of any element

domain group of magnetic atoms

electromagnet temporary magnet created when an electric current flows through a conductor

electron tiny particle in an atom that travels around the nucleus

magma melted rock found beneath the surface of earth

magnetic field area around a magnet that has the power to attract magnetic metals

magnetite a hard, black rock found in earth that attracts iron. Magnetite is also known as lodestone.

magnetosphere magnetic field extending into space around a planet or star

nucleus centre of an atom. A nucleus is made up of neutrons and protons.

pivot point on which something turns or balances

pole one of the two ends of a magnet. A pole can also be the top or bottom part of a planet.

repel push apart. Like poles of magnets repel each other.

temporary lasting only a short time

FIND OUT MORE

Books

Electricity and Magnetism (Tabletop Scientist series), Steve Parker (Heinemann Library 2005)

Magnets (Do It Yourself series), Rachel Lynette (Heinemann Library, 2008)

Magnets: Sticking Together, Wendy Sadler (Raintree, 2006)

What's the Attraction?, Elizabeth Raum (Raintree, 2006)

Websites

www.bbc.co.uk/schools/ks2bitesize
Click on "Science", then on "Physical processes", then "Magnets and springs activity" for a fun way to see how magnets work.

http://news.bbc/co.uk/cbbcnews
Enter "magnets" in the Search field to find out how magnets have been used and have been in the news.

INDEX